T0064157

Ingredients

A Collection of Motivational Ingredients to Facilitate your Every Success in This Journey Called Life

TO WHOM MUCH IS GIVEN MUCH IS REQUIRED

There Is Nothing You Can Not Do,
Only Things You Have Not Done Yet.

MARK ROBINSON

ISBN: 978-1-4907-1239-0 (sc)
ISBN: 978-1-4907-1240-6 (e)

Trafford rev. 04/08/2014

 www.trafford.com

North America & international
toll-free: 1 888 232 4444 (USA & Canada)
fax: 812 355 4082

INGREDIENTS

Accountability
Adaptability
Attitude
Awareness
Belief
Character
Commitment
Compassion
Competent
Confidence
Courage
Dedication
Dependability
Desire
Determination
Diligence
Discipline
Effort
Encouragement
Endurance
Ethics
Flexibility
Focus
Gratitude
Honesty
Hope

Jesus Christ

Humility
Integrity
Knowledge
Leadership
Motivation
Obedience
Patience
Perseverance
Persistence
Reliability
Respect
Responsibility
Resiliency
Sacrifice
Self awareness
Self esteem
Sincerity
Spirituality
Tenacity
Trustworthiness
Understanding
Values
Vision
Willingness
Wisdom

Fruits of the Spirit

Preface

As I look back over my life, I can see the development, and lack of the ingredients I have outlined in this book during various stages of my life; even to the present. I have learned that these ingredients are essential ingredients necessary to obtain success in all facets of my life; (spiritual, personal, relationships, family, financial, business).

When I was a child, the development of these ingredients began to unfold. I was unaware at that time of the plan that would mold and shape me, as I journeyed through life's challenges, into the man God created me to be.

As I look back over my life, I can see when the development of certain ingredients enabled me to mature to the next level of development. I can also see when the lack of certain ingredients inhibited me from growing beyond my present circumstances. I have determined that the effectiveness of some ingredients depended on the existence of some of the other ingredients. Many of these ingredients have similarities in acquisition and application. It is my belief that the inter-connectedness of many of these ingredients will be revealed to you, and you will understand the importance of acquiring all the ingredients for your journey towards success in life. On your journey, you WILL encounter adversity.

> **These things I have spoken to you, that in me you might have peace. In the world you shall have tribulation: but be of good cheer; I have overcome the world. John 16:33 (KJV)**

If you are not going anywhere, nothing can get in your way.

Now that all these INGREDIENTS have been gathered, some still need to be added, and completed by the Holy Ghost, I can begin to fulfill my purpose for which God has created me for. I am not perfect. Every now and then, I have to stir up my ingredients. The pot continues to simmer.

I am not done yet. There are ingredients that still can be added. Life is a journey, with a destination.

Success is a result of planning. Success just does not happen. Success occurs when opportunity meets preparation. Success is a process. Success is not a destination, it is a journey. Success is not a failure but learning from failure.

I was inspired by the Spirit of God to write this book to help you achieve the success you desire in life. The quotes, messages, and scriptures in this book are designed to empower you, equip you, and to motivate you as you journey along the highways and bi-ways, the mountains and the valleys towards spiritual development and personal success in your life. May God Bless you and keep you.

Ingredients

$\mathcal{A}$ccountability:

Makes you liable to being called to account for you actions; answerable.

Everything that we do along this journey called life to achieve success is governed by some kind of rule of engagement, guidelines, or laws. They dictate our behavior on the journey. There are governing entities that we must answer to. Accepting accountability helps us to keep on our toes. When we know that we always have to answer to someone, we are more inclined to do things the right way the first time. There is no higher entity than the Father. God created the heavens and the earth, and the laws that we are all held accountable to. When our actions are not in agreement with those who have authority over us, or who place enough trust in us to give us some authority, we lose our position. God wants us to be accountable so we do not lose our position in His Kingdom. We have to be accountable to ourselves as well as others. We cannot escape accountability. We know what the person in the mirror is capable of. When we accept accountability we accept responsibility for our behaviors that make us fall short of our capability. Accountability helps you harness your weakness, so you can fulfill your capacity.

> **Now we know that whatever the law says, it says to those who are under the law, so that every mouth may be silenced and the whole world held accountable to God. Romans 3:19 (NIV)**

> **Jesus told his disciples: "There is a rich man whose manager was accused of wasting his possessions. So he called him in and asked him,'What is this I hear about you? Give an account of your management, because you cannot be manager any longer." Luke 16:1-2**

> **Nothing in all creation is hidden from God's sight. Everything is uncovered and laid bare before the eyes of him to whom we must give account. Hebrews 4:13 (NIV)**

Adaptability:

Capable of adapting or of being adapted. Ability to make suitable to a specific use or situation. Ability to accommodate, adjust, conform, or fit.

Adaptability is a requirement if we are to overcome challenges and obstacles that we must face whenever we are confronted with unfamiliar surroundings. As you can see from the scriptures below, it is just as important to know when and where to adapt as it is to have the ability. When we find ourselves confronted by circumstances that are unfavorable towards the realization of our vision, we don't adapt, conform, or fit in to that environment, we become diligent in our pursuit of our destiny. As we pursue our purpose in life revealed through our vision, it should be expected of ourselves to be at least above those who have no vision or whose vision is misguided. Your ability to adapt to your environment and overcome your circumstances will determine your accessibility to the next level of your journey.

> **"Therefore this is what the Sovereign Lord says: You have been more unruly than the nations around you and have not followed my decrees or kept my laws. You have not even conformed to the standards of the nations around you. Ezekiel 5:7 (NIV)**
>
> **And we know that in all things God works for the good of those who love him, who have been called according to his purpose. For those God foreknew he also predestined to be conformed to the likeness of his Son, that he might be the firstborn among many brothers. And those he predestined, he also called; those he called, he also justified; those he justified, he also glorified. Romans 8:28-30**

Attitude:

A state of mind or a feeling; disposition.

There is a great deal of emphasis and significance placed on attitude, and for a good reason. I have found both the old and new me within the scriptures. I have lived through the consequences of the wrong attitude, and now reap the benefits of the right attitude. The right attitude is so important to your success on your journey through life. Your attitude is an expression of your emotions of the heart. The things that are in our heart are the things that we feel the strongest toward. The things we dwell on the most in our minds becomes embedded in our heart. Our emotions influence our actions. Our actions determine our outcomes and the level of success we ultimately achieve. Therefore, making attitude very important to our success in life. Our attitude, that is, our emotions, how and what we feel in our heart, and our thoughts determine our actions. We must exercise wisdom and discernment when deciding who and what events in our lives we let influence our thoughts. We must be teachable and seek understanding of the lessons we learn on our journey through life. Your actions will reflect whether you have the right attitude or the wrong attitude. There are many points of view in which the bible approaches attitude. Your altitude is determined by your attitude. A humble attitude will allow you to fulfill your ultimate purpose in life.

> **Teach me thy way, O Lord; I will walk in thy truth: unite my heart to fear thy name. Psalms 86:11 (KJV)**

> **I the Lord search the heart and examine the mind, to reward a man according to his conduct, according to what his deeds deserve. Jeremiah 17:10 (NIV)**

> **Keep your heart with all diligence, for out of it *spring* the issues of life. Put away from you a deceitful mouth, and put perverse lips far from you. (Proverbs 4:23-24)**

$\mathcal{A}$wareness:

Having knowledge of; State of elementary or undifferentiated consciousness

There are many things that we must have awareness of. Therefore there are many questions most of ask ourselves. Questions like: Who am I? Where did I come from? Why am I here? Where am I going? These have to do with self awareness which I will address later in the book. There are other elements that it is essential we have awareness of; like our environment or surroundings, who is in our "Inner Circle" or support team. If you know the answers to these two questions, you will be able to determine if you are on the right path, or have the necessary people around you for achieving success that comes with awareness of who you really are, your purpose, and destiny in life. It is important to have awareness of the environment you are surrounded by. You should know whether or not it is conducive to your success; can it support your vision? What challenges does it present that you have to be prepared for? Success occurs when opportunity meets preparation.

> **And Moses sent them to spy out the land of Canaan . . . And see the land, what it is; and the people that dwelleth there, whether they be strong or weak, few or many; And what the land is they dwell in, whether it be good or bad . . . And what the land is, whether it be fat or lean, whether there be wood therein, or not. Num 13: 17-20 (KJV)**

$\mathcal{B}$elief:

Something believed or accepted as true, especially a particular tenet or a body of tenets accepted by a group of persons.

When I was a child what I believed in depended on the source of knowledge that my beliefs were founded on (parents, family, friends, teachers, the world, etc . . .). What I came to believe in influenced my thoughts and perceptions of the world around me and my ability to function in that world. Everyone and everything that influenced my beliefs were not always the best person or the best thing to base my beliefs on. They did not always lead me to see and believe in my ability to succeed. As I journeyed through life, I learned to develop my own beliefs based on how I perceived the world through my own experiences. What I believed in became the motivation that directed my thoughts and perceptions about the world in which I lived, and about myself. What you think about the most becomes embedded in your heart. You work hard to achieve success in the things you believe in your heart, and you endure criticism because you believe these things down in your heart.

If the people, places, and things you believed in as a child misled you to believe that you could not overcome your challenges in life, understand that you are no longer dependent upon them to determine what you believe in. You must believe in yourself! Learn to know who your "self" is. As you journey on this road called life, remember that what you believe in is determined by the way you think. The way you think is based on the information you receive in your mind. The only way to change the way you think is to receive new information. New information is processed in your mind and enters your heart. It then becomes what you believe and impacts your feelings. What you believe and how you feel impact your thoughts. Your thoughts determine your actions. Receive new information to change the way you think and believe so you can change the way you act. People tend to be in their life what the most important people in their life think about them.

Then God said, "Let us make man in our own image, in our likeness . . .
So God created man in His own image, in the image of God He created him; Genesis 1:26-27 (NIV)

For therefore we both labor and suffer reproach, because we trust in the living God, who is the Savior of all men, especially of those that believe. 1 Timothy 4:10 (KJV)

Dear friends, do not believe every spirit, but test the spirits to see whether they are from God, because many false prophets have gone out into the world. 1 John 4:1 (NIV)

"Do not conform any longer to the pattern of this world, but be transformed by the renewing of your mind. Then you will be able to test and approve what God's will is—His good, pleasing and perfect will." Romans 12:2 (NIV)

Ingredients

Character:

The combination of qualities or features that distinguishes a person from another.

We are created in God's image. What's inside of us is Godlike. It is the character inside of us that distinguish us from every other person. <u>Knowing</u> that God Almighty is inside of each and every one of us should empower us to conquer our adversities in life. Character is what's inside you. It is what others see in you that attracts them to you. Good or bad character, both will ultimately distinguish you from the crowd. But to have no character at all will disassociate you from a crowd of anything at all. People buy into your character. The way you conduct yourself is an indication or outward expression of what's inside you. When faced with adversity, it's what's inside you that leads you to triumph over it. Whatever measure of character you have has been developed by going through many of the negative experiences you have had to overcome. It is not enough to just survive adversity, trials, and tribulation, you must overcome and triumph over them. Trials in life develop character. You must overcome challenges in order to go to a higher level in life. Good character is when you are who you are all the time; even when there is no one watching. Character is consistent behavior and attitude. A man of God's character says what he means and means what he says. Your help is in you. Understanding of what is in you and who you are in Christ Jesus is the key to good character and to unlock the door to all that God has for you.

> **And he who is the Glory of Israel will not lie, nor will he change his mind, for he is not human that he should change his mind! 1 Sam 15:29 (NLT)**

> **Blessed is the man who perseveres over trials, because when he has stood the test, he will receive the crown of life that God has promised to those who love him. James 1:12 (NIV)**

> **Therefore since we have been justified through faith, we have peace with God through our Lord Jesus Christ, through whom**

we have gained access by faith into this grace in which we now stand. And we rejoice in the hope of the glory of God. Not only so, but we also rejoice in our sufferings, because we know that suffering produces perseverance; perseverance, character; and character, hope. Rom 5:1-4 (NIV)

Do not be misled: Bad company corrupts good character. 1 Cor 15:33 (NIV)

All that you need to be, you already are. Character is Developed When You Endure, Persevere, and Overcome Trials. How I live my life when no one else is watching will determine the measure of success I have when the whole world is watching.

Commitment:

The state of being bound emotionally or intellectually to someone or something.

In order to be successful at achieving your desired goals you must have commitment. As you are walking out your steps towards success in any area of your life, you are going to face some discouragement. There is always going to be someone or something that tells you to give up, you can't do that. How committed to your dreams are you? Each level of success is going to require a greater level of commitment. The higher you go up, the higher your commitment has to be. The commitment required to overcome discouragement on one level will not be sufficient enough to overcome discouragement at higher levels. How high do you want to go?

Turn that discouragement into motivation. When I was a little boy around nine or ten years old, we used to play sandlot football . . . one block against another block. I learned then that I was very good at football. One day I told my grandmother that I was good at football. She told me you're not as good as your father was. That was not what I wanted to hear. I told her that I was, but she would not believe me. At that time I committed myself to becoming the best football player I could be. I believed that the only way I could show my grandmother that I was a good football player was to play on TV in the NFL one day. I went on to become a great football player and earned a scholarship to play football at the college level. I soon learned that I was good at the college level as well. I also learned that it required a greater commitment to play at the top of my game at that level. Because I lacked the commitment to prepare myself mentally to play at that level, I never made it to the NFL. It was not because I lacked the ability and talent, but because I lacked the commitment. Your commitment will reflect your desire to be successful. Success cannot be achieved if you do not apply yourself.

Ruth had the kind of commitment that would not allow her to give up on what she believed in no matter who or what tried to discourage her.

> But Ruth replied, "Don't urge me to leave you or to turn back from you. Where you go I will go, and where you stay I will stay. Your people will be my people and your God my God. Where you die I will die, and there I will be buried. May the Lord deal with me, be it ever so severely, if anything but death separate you and me. When Naomi realized that Ruth was determined to go with her, she stopped urging her. Ruth 1:16-18 (NIV)

Compassion:

Deep awareness of suffering of another coupled with the wish to relieve it.

Compassion is an emotion that compels and motivates one to empower those in less favorable circumstances. It positions us emotionally and mentally to recognize and to feel someone else's' pain. A sign of a successful person is that when you see or hear of others suffering, your heart falters because you want to see them achieve success in their life by overcoming adverse circumstances, and you want to help.

> **Rescue those being led away to death; hold back those staggering toward slaughter. Proverbs 24:11 (NKJV)**

> **At this my body is racked with pain, pangs seize me, like those of a woman in labor; I am staggered by what I hear, I am bewildered by what I see. Isaiah 21:3 (NIV)**

> **Carry each other's burdens, and in this way you will fulfill the law of Christ. 6:2 (NIV)**

Competence:

The state of being adequately or well qualified; ability

Competence is the ingredient that gives you confidence to conquer all challenges. When you know you have the skill to accomplish a task, you believe in yourself. You know you have the ability to do what it takes to get the job done. What gives me competence? Knowing that I was created in the image of God and in His likeness assures me that I am competent to handle any challenge I am faced with. Therefore I am confident that I can get the job done. Your help is in you. Understanding of what is in you and who you are in Christ Jesus is the key to unlock the door to all that God has for you and will give you competence and confidence.

> **Then God said, "Let Us make man in Our image, according to Our likeness; Gen 1:26 (NKJV)**
>
> **Not that we are competent in ourselves to claim anything for ourselves, but our competence comes from God. 2 Cor 3:5 (NIV)**

Ingredients

Confidence:

A feeling of assurance, especially of self-assurance. The state or quality of being certain.

Confidence and competence are closely related. When you have confidence in your abilities, which comes from knowing who you are in Jesus Christ, and live your life according to the knowledge of who you are, you develop competence. You feel more secure within yourself and more competent to accomplish the goals you set for yourself. Confidence in yourself allows you to take risks on your journey towards success. Confidence should not be mistaken for, or replace faith. If there were no risks in life, you would not need to have faith.

The devil will try to destroy your confidence by causing you to doubt God's spoken words over your life. He will try to discourage you and he will use those closest to you. He does not care whose lives he destroy along the way. He does not want you to succeed or fulfill your destiny.

> **Do not be afraid of sudden terror, nor of trouble from the wicked when it comes; For the Lord will be your confidence, and will keep your foot from being caught. Pr 3:25-26 (NKJV)**

> **We are confident in all this because of our great trust in God through Christ. 2 Co 3:4 (NLV)**

> **Therefore do not throw away your confidence, which has great reward. Heb 10:35 (ESV)**

> **I can do all things through Christ who strengthens me. Php 4:13 (NKJV)**

> **Finally, my brethren, be strong in the Lord, and in the power of his might.**

Put on the whole armor of God, that you may be able to stand against the wiles of the devil.

For we wrestle not against flesh and blood, but against principalities, against powers, against the rulers of the darkness of this world, against spiritual wickedness in high places.

Courage:

The state or quality of mind or spirit that enables one to face danger, fear, or vicissitudes with self-possession and resolution; bravery.

You have to have courage to face your fears. Most of our fears are those hidden deep inside us. Those are the fears that require the most courage. Fear of the unknown, fear of exposing our own inadequacies, fear of change, fear of what others will think about us, fear of rejection, and fear of failure are just a few of the many fears we encounter in life. But when we understand, trust, and believe that the Lord thy God is with us our fears begin to disappear. We develop confidence and the courage to conquer our fears. It is not just conquering our fears that requires courage, but breaking strongholds that develop as a result of generational curses. It takes courage to break those strongholds that manifest in the form of barriers and limitations in our lives. Those strongholds create giant obstacles to your destiny. It takes the courage that Caleb had in the bible to overcome what might appear as giant obstacles and limitations.

> **Be strong and of a good courage, fear not, nor be afraid of them: for the Lord thy God, he it is that doth go with thee; he will not fail thee, nor forsake thee. Dut 31:6 (NKJV)**
>
> **. . . Take courage as you fulfill your duties, and may the Lord be with those who do what is right. 2 Ch 19:11 (NLT)**
>
> **And Caleb stilled the people before Moses, and said, Let us go up at once, and posses it; for we are well able to overcome it. Num 13:30 (KJV)**

Dedication:

Selfless devotion to a particular course of action or thought.

If we are to achieve the success we desire towards our goals we must be dedicated wholeheartedly to those goals. We make difficult or prolong the achievement of our goals if our heart is not in it. God adds the reward to the things we wholeheartedly dedicate ourselves to. God will bring forth the victory over our adversities in life when we have been dedicated to what He has called us to do without giving in to distractions. We must be focused and not deceived into believing that there is a better way. We must keep our hearts pure and our wholehearted dedication to what God has called us to achieve. What you are going to be tomorrow, you are already working on it today.

> **Remember, O Lord, how I have walked before you faithfully and with wholehearted devotion and have done what is good in your eyes. 2 Kings 20:3 (NIV)**

> **I am saying this for your own good, not to restrict you, but that you may live a right way in undivided devotion to the Lord. 1 Co 7:35 (NIV)**

> **But I am afraid that just as Eve was deceived by the serpent's cunning, your minds may somehow be led astray from your sincere and pure devotion to Christ. 2 Co 11:3 (NIV)**

Ingredients

Dependability:

Trustworthy. Reliable.

It is important to be dependable, trustworthy, and faithful in whatever we are given responsibility over. Those who give you that responsibility are depending, trusting, and have faith in you to be a good steward over what they have made you responsible of. Those who you are responsible for are also depending on you to be a role model and leader. There is always someone watching you; watching the way you do things, and assessing your dependability. Whether it is those who have authority over you or those who you have been given authority over. God wants to establish leaders He can depend on to be over His people. Some of us will become leaders of a great number of people, others just a few. Regardless of how much you are given responsibility over, you must able to be depended on. If you are faithful over a little God will bless you with a lot. Your level of responsibility will reflect your level of dependability.

> **Moreover, look for able men from all the people, men who fear God, who are trustworthy and hate a bribe, and place such men over the people as chiefs of thousands, of hundreds, of fifties, and of tens. Ex 18:21 (ESV)**

> **Well done, my good servant! His master replied. Because you have been trustworthy in a very small matter, take charge of ten cities. Luke 19:17 (NIV)**

> **Moreover it is required in stewards, that a man be found faithful. 1 Cor. 4:2 (KJV)**

esire:

To wish or long for; want.

Desire has to have the proper motivation. The things that we desire
are the source of our strongest motivation. Whatever we desire the
most is what's in our hearts; it's where we focus all of our efforts,
energy, attention, time, thoughts, emotions, and resources. We become
consumed by what is in our hearts. We all have a desire to achieve
success in life, or at least to achieve success at something. We must guard
our hearts and be mindful of the things we desire.

> **May he grant your heart's desires and make all your plans
> succeed. Psa 20:4 (NLT)**

> **For as he thinketh in his heart, so is he . . . Pr 23:7 (KJV)**

> **For what will it profit a man if he gains the whole world and
> forfeits his life? Or what shall a man give in return for his life?
> Mat. 16;26 (ESV)**

Determination:

Firmness of purpose; resolve. A fixed intention or resolution.

> **Blessed is the man who walks not in the counsel of the ungodly,
> nor stands in the path of the sinners, nor sits in the seat of the
> scournful; But his delight is in the law of the Lord, and in His
> law he meditates day and night. He is like a tree planted by the
> rivers of water, that brings it's fruit in it's season, whose leaf
> also shall not whither; And whatever he does shall prosper. The
> ungodly are not so, but are like the chaff which the wind blows
> away. Psalms 1:1-4 (NKJV)**

This is a man that is determined and focused on his purpose He cannot
be persuaded or deterred from achieving his goal. Determination is a
key ingredient for success. Without it we give up on our desires at the
slightest confrontation, conflict or adversity. When we make a decision
to achieve or to accomplish a goal, we must make up in our minds
that no matter what, we will see it through. Conflicts and adversity
will confront us and appear before us in many forms, vices, and
fashions. Life altering events may occur in our lives that challenges our
determination. But often times our determination is tested by those who
try to discourage us by telling us not to do what we set out to do or that
we can't do it. We are challenged by those who are going nowhere and
don't want to see us go anywhere either. We must stay determined in the
face of adversity no matter what form it confronts us in. Determination
is fortified knowing that we can do all things through Christ who
strengthens us (Php 4:13). We must be planted firmly in our conviction
to achieve the success we are determined to achieve or else we will be
easily discouraged and blown away like the chaff.

One should remember that opposition comes to test your resolve.
Obstacles show you your weakness and provoke you to be creative.
Success and failure many times has to do with the ability to outlast your
opposition. Determination is a tough minded, strong willed disposition
toward a desired end. If you are determined you will find a way to

win. Failure is not an option. You summons your gifts, talents, friends and your faith with the knowledge that after the storm I will still be standing . . . I am determined.

-Michael Pitts

The race is not always to the swift, nor the battle to the strong . . . Ecc. 9:11 (KJV); But to those who have determination.

Ingredients

$\mathcal{D}$iligence:

Earnest, persistent application to an undertaking.

Diligence is a key ingredient on this journey called life. You are always going to encounter opposition on the path to success. There are going to be times when you are tempted to give up on your goals, and pursue other things that are designed to distract you. But if we diligently stay on course, and remain persistent, we will reach our goal. There are times in life when you just want to give up; you become discouraged. That's when diligence is needed the most. You see, diligence has a reward. We can not give up on our dreams and desires. Success comes to those who are diligent in their pursuit.

> **And it shall come to pass, if thou shall hearken diligently unto the voice of the Lord thy God, to observe and to do all His commandments which I command thee this day, that the Lord thy God will set thee on high above all nations of the earth: And all these blessing shall come on thee, and overtake thee, if thou shall hearken unto the voice of the Lord thy God. Dut. 28:1-2 (KJV)**

> **He becomes poor that deals with a slack hand: but the hand of the diligent makes rich. Prov 10:4 (KJV)**

> **But without faith it is impossible to please Him: for he that comes to God must believe that He is, and that He is a rewarder of them that diligently seek Him. Heb. 11:6 (KJV)**

Discipline:

Controlled behavior resulting from disciplinary training; self-control. A system of rules of conduct or method of practice. The trait of being well behaved.

Discipline produces a mentality of "sticktuativeness"; a belief system that says "I will not give up", that is developed as a result of experiencing consequences from past actions. Those consequences may have been negative or positive. Over time they establish you and help you to stay focused. You see, discipline in your life and on your journey will secure your future success. Discipline takes practice. In some cases it takes years of training before you can acquire the discipline necessary to respond to adversity in a controlled behavior. Discipline, as defined, gives you training essential to dealing with the troubles you will face on your journey. It equips you to stay focused on the things needed to achieve the success you desire. You can rest during the storms you may face because you have the discipline to not allow them to overtake you and to cause you to break your focus. Men fail because of broken focus. Discipline is forced obedience until it becomes a habit.

> **Blessed is the man whom you discipline, O Lord, and whom you teach out of your law, to give him rest from days of trouble . . . Ps 94:12-13 (ESV)**

> **Fear of the Lord is the foundation of true knowledge, but fools despise wisdom and discipline. Pr. 1:7 (NLT)**

> **Death is the reward of an undisciplined life; your foolish decisions trap you in a dead end. Pr. 5:23 (The Message)**

Effort:

The use of physical or mental energy to accomplish something.

Success in life does not come without effort. You have to apply yourself both physically and mentally to achieve the success you desire in life. Success without effort really adds no value to your accomplishment. You can never hold on to success that has no real meaning to you. We expend too much effort and energy chasing after the wrong things in life. You should make your efforts worth your while!

> **Better to have one handful with quietness than two handfuls with hard work and chasing the wind. Ecc 4:6 (NLT)**

Find your purpose and focus your efforts on it. Do not look to the left or the right! Your efforts will lead to success when you have a purpose for what you are doing.

> **This is the case of a man who is all alone, without a child or a brother, yet who works hard to gain as much wealth as he can. But then asks himself, Who am I working for? Why am I giving up so much pleasure now? It is all so meaningless and depressing. Ecc. 4:8 (NLT)**

When you focus your efforts on gaining the wrong things for the wrong reasons, it creates greater problems than the ones you began with. You should focus your efforts on things worth while and meaningful!

Success cannot be achieved if you don't apply yourself. Achieving the success you desire is the result of planning and strategies. Success just does not happen. Success is a process. Success is not failure, but learning from failure. On the journey to achieving the success you desire will be many obstacles, challenges, adversities, and adversaries.

Encouragement:

The expression of approval and support. The act of giving hope or support to someone. The feeling of being encouraged.

Encouragement is an essential ingredient to add to your recipe for success. It is necessary for you to not only be encouraged but to be an encouragement to others around you.

> **One day near Horesh, David received the news that Saul was on the way to Ziph to search for him and kill him. Jonathan went to find David and encouraged him to stay strong in his faith in God. "Don't be afraid," Jonathan reassured him. "My father will never find you! You are going to be the king of Irael, and I will be next to you, as my father, Saul, is well aware." I Samuel 23: 15-17 (NLT)**

When you want to give up and quit, when you feel like you've lost all hope, when you feel like your back is up against the wall and there is no place else to turn, a word of encouragement can make all the difference to motivate you or someone you do not want see give up on their dreams. My grandmother used to always tell me, "Don't give up Mark, God has a plan for you!" I did not know what she meant or what that plan was back at the times when I truly needed to hear those words of encouragement, but they would always provide me with hope. Those words of encouragement spoke life into my seemingly hopeless circumstances. They kept me from totally giving up and always seeking that plan.

> **Therefore encourage one another and build one another up, just as you are doing.**
> 1 Thess. 5:11 (ESV)

THERE IS NOTHING YOU CANNOT DO ONLY THINGS YOU HAVE NOT DONE YET

Ingredients

If you have tried to do something and you have failed, you are not a failure. You simply have not tried hard enough to be successful at what you desire. If you desire to be successful at something, and you are willing to do what it takes to be successful at it, you will be successful. Do not give up and do not be discouraged. You are not a failure. Failure often times precedes success. In order to achieve success, you must be determined and committed to success. Success comes with a price tag called sacrifice. Are you willing to make sacrifices to achieve the success you desire?

*E*ndurance:

The power to withstand hardship or stress. A state of surviving; remaining alive.

Sometimes you have to outlast your present circumstances. Some victories are not the result of overcoming adversity or defeating an adversary, but outlasting them. You have to press through and wait it out. Everyday the sun doesn't shine in our lives. Sometimes it rains. We go through different seasons in our life. We enjoy happiness, pleasure, and triumphant victories during the sunny seasons in our life. But when it's a rainy season, and the storms come, and the winds blow, we go through struggles and trials and tribulations. That's when we have to have endurance. You see, every since the beginning of time, every time it rains, every time there has been a storm, the sun has never failed to come back out. We have to endure the rainy seasons and the hard times and stress that comes with them, knowing that the sun will always return. Once you have endured the storms, you will have gained from the experience, and be equipped with the knowledge and ability to survive it when ever it comes your way again.

> **But he that shall endure unto the end, the same shall be saved. Mat 24:13 (KJV).**

> **Blessed is the man that endureth temptation: for when he is tried, he shall receive the crown of life, which the lord hath promised to them that love him. James 1:12 (KJV).**

The Message bible states it like this: **Anyone who meets a testing challenge head-on and manages to stick it out is mighty fortunate. For such persons loyally in love with God, the reward is life and more life.**

"All daring and courage, all iron endurance of misfortune—make for a finer, nobler type of manhood." Theodore Roosevelt

Ingredients

*E*thics:

A set of principles of right conduct. A theory or a system of moral values.

Everyone must have a personal code of ethics by which they stand on and live by; a conviction or belief that they will not compromised when faced with adversity and temptation. That conviction or belief becomes the standard by which every action, behavior, or decision is judged. You must have faith in those ethics and principles when confronted by the pressures of life that could cause you to compromise your beliefs. The code of ethics or principles that you live by govern and determine the choices you make in life, family, on the job, and relationships. Most businesses or professions have a code of ethics that regulates the behavior of those who work in them. When those codes of ethics are violated there are usually negative consequences that follow. The same should hold true in our personal lives. We must stand firm on our convictions and beliefs; never compromising them without expecting negative consequences.

> **Therefore put on the full armor of God, so that when the day of evil comes, you may be able to stand your ground, and after you have done everything to stand, to stand. Stand firm then, with the belt of truth buckled around your waist, with the breastplate of righteousness in place, and with your feet fitted with the readiness that comes from the gospel of peace. In addition to all this, take up the shield of faith, with which you can extinguish all the flaming arrows of the evil one. Take the helmet of salvation and the sword of the spirit, which is the word of God. Eph 6: 13-17 (NIV)**

> **And if it seem evil unto you to serve the LORD, choose you this day whom ye will serve; whether the gods which your fathers served that were on the other side of the flood, or the gods of the Amorites, in whose land ye dwell: but as for me and my house, we will serve the LORD. Joshua 24: 15**

$\mathcal{F}$aith:

The theological virtue defined as secure belief in God and a trusting acceptance of God's will.

For we walk by faith not by sight: 2 Corinthians 5:7

Now faith is the substance of things hoped for, the evidence of things not seen. Hebrews 11:1

But without faith it is impossible to please him: for he that cometh to God must believe that he is, and that he is a rewarder of them that diligently seek him. Hebrews 11:6

Faith has to be developed. It is not easy to come by without having been through some uncertain and challenging times in your life. It is easy to pat yourself on the back when you escape the consequences of situations in your life that could have been impossible to recover from. But, be faced with something you cannot get yourself out of; no decision you make will be the one to pull you through, and you know for certain that the situation is hopeless, and yet when things are darkest in your life they some how turn out in your favor. That is how faith is developed. That is when you begin to walk by faith and not by sight. That is when you begin to believe and trust in God. Faith is what keeps you moving forward even in the face of adversity. It keeps you from giving up when things get difficult. God wants you to diligently seek him for the things you cannot see possible in the natural. Trust in God and he will reward you with the things you hope for.

Ingredients

Flexibility:

The property of being flexible. The quality of being adaptable or variable. Ability to adjust readily to different conditions; Bends and snaps back readily without breaking. Making or willing to make concessions.

On our journey through life, we sometimes find ourselves faced with different environments. These environments sometimes challenge the way we think, feel, believe, and behave. Life presents us with many changes along the journey. It is then when our flexibility is tested. Whether it is in our personal life, relationships, or on the job, flexibility is an essential ingredient for success. At various times we are push to the brink of giving up; have reached a breaking point. Flexibility allows you to bend but not break. It is at that breaking point that we exhibit our greatest strength. The strength that is in each and every one of us causes us to break free of that person, place, thing, situation, circumstance, or thought that is taking us to the brink of giving up and launches us into a new level. It takes us to a new season where we have a renewed strength, a fresh perspective, and a passion to strive for continued growth and success.

Anything that does not change you is unnecessary in your life.

"We are moving from an Industrial Age built on gears and sweat to an Information Age, demanding skills and learning and flexibility."—Bill Clinton

ocus:

The concentration of attention or energy on something; Maximum clarity or distinctness of an idea; Special emphasis attached to something.

When you know where you are going in life, or what it is that you desire to achieve success in, it is important that you have focus. The world around you is designed to distract you from your purpose. You will fail when your focus is broken. You must continue to keep your eyes on the prize; not look to the left or the right. When your focus is broken you can easily be distracted and led astray. You can be convinced that the grass is greener on the other side, or that you can achieve success faster if you do it another way other than the way you know is the right way. Focus on the goal with maximum clarity of the destination and you will be able to withstand the efforts of those who wish to deter and hinder you from achieving the success you desire in life. The WORD tells me that Satan comes to kill, steal, and destroy.

> **Therefore, my dear brothers, stand firm. Let nothing move you. Always give yourselves fully to the work of the Lord, because you know that your labor in the Lord is not in vain. 1 Cor. 15:58 (NIV)**

> **Jesus replied, "No one who puts his hand to the plow and looks back is fit for service in the kingdom of God." Luke 9:62 (NIV)**

> **Do not swerve to the right or the left; keep foot from evil. Prov. 4:27 (NIV)**

> **Enter ye in at the strait gate: for wide is the gate, and broad is the way, that leadeth to destruction, and many there be which go in thereat: Because strait is the gate, and narrow is the way, which leadeth unto life, and few there be that find it. Mat 7:13-14 (KJV)**

Ingredients

ratitude:

A feeling of thankfulness and appreciation.

Gratitude is an ingredient that when others know it exist in you, through your open expression of it, they do not mind lending you a helping hand. Gratitude will unleash favor in your life.

If it was not for God's grace where would I be? I owe Him so much. I could not begin to thank Him enough. I am so grateful to my Lord and Savior Jesus Christ for His sacrifice, obedience, willingness, commitment, faithfulness, love, understanding . . . I could go on and on about things I am grateful for. A reason for gratitude is the thing that is easy to identify. All you have to do is take a deep breath. The air you breathe is God's. Every day that you awake, clothed in your right mind, in good health with full use of your limbs is a reason to exhibit gratitude, thankfulness, and appreciation toward God. If you have shelter, food, water, clothes, you have more than millions of children and people in this world.

> **Enter into his gates with thanksgiving, and into his courts with praise: be thankful unto him, and bless his name. Ps 100:4 (KJV)**

Guidance:

Direction or advice as to a decision or course of action. The act of guiding or showing the way. The act of setting and holding a course.

What ever it is you want to achieve in life, it is important to know someone who knows how to get there and will give you guidance; someone to plot the course for you, so you do not get lost on the journey. I have learned that when I do things without proper guidance (Jesus), I usually make bad decisions in regards to the direction I should go. It does not matter what area of your life it is, you must have accurate and precise guidance. Without guidance, we learn from the experiences of traveling down the wrong road. They say that experience is the best teacher. I say that experience is a good teacher. But the best teacher is the one who has already learned from their experiences and can teach you so you do not have to have the experience.

> **I will instruct thee and teach thee in the way which thou shalt go: I will guide thee with mine eye. Psalms 32:8 (KJV)**
>
> **Trust in the LORD with all thine heart; and lean not unto thine own understanding. In all thy ways acknowledge him, and he shall direct thy paths. Prov. 3:5-6 (KJV)**
>
> **Jesus saith unto him, I am the way, the truth, and the life: no man cometh unto the Father, but by me. Jhn 14:6 (KJV)**
>
> **Where no counsel is, the people fall: but in the multitude of counselors there is safety. Prov. 11:14 (KJV)**

Ingredients

$\mathcal{H}$onesty:

The quality of being honest. Truthfulness; sincerity.

> **No account of this money was required from the construction supervisors, because they were honest and trustworthy men. 2 Kings 12:15 (NLT)**

> **He that speaketh truth showeth forth righteousness: but a false witness deceit. Prov. 12:17 (KJV)**

I have found that honesty is the best policy. There is no wasted energy or effort when it comes to being honest. It's just natural for an honest person. Honesty is an ingredient that can reward you with extreme favor among men. Honesty frees you from the stress of having to remember all the things you have been dishonest about. It takes a lot of energy to remember each lie you told and not get entangled by the web of lies you weave. When honesty is a part of who you are, people recognize that quality in you and present you with opportunities that lead to the success you desire in life. It is simple; just tell the truth. "The truth shall set you free."

Hope:

A specific instance of feeling hopeful. The general feeling that some desire will be fulfilled. Grounds for feeling hopeful about the future.

> *For as the rain and snow come down from heaven, and do not*
> *return there but water the earth, making it bring forth and*
> *sprout, giving seed to the sower and bread to the eater,*
> *So shall my word be that goes out from my mouth; it shall not*
> *return to me empty, but it shall accomplish that which I purpose,*
> *and shall succeed in the thing for which I sent it.*
> *Isa. 55:10-11 (KJV)*

> *To every thing there is a season, and a time to every purpose*
> *under the heaven: Ecc. 3:1 (KJV)*

Hope is developed when we experience adversity in our life, family, marriage, jobs, finances; you name it. Hope is an essential ingredient. It is what motivates us to hold on, endure, outlast, and overcome the adverse circumstances we encounter on our journey towards success. Hope comes by hearing a word from God. Hearing a word from God activates our faith and breathes hope into our circumstances. Hope keeps us moving forward towards that season and time in which God has purposed for us to achieve the success we hope for in our life.

Humility:

The quality or state of being humble; freedom from pride and arrogance; lowliness of mind.

One of the most essential ingredients for success in your life is humility. Without humility, destruction, chaos, frustration, pain, sorrow, and suffering will be the results in your life. The opposite of humility is of course pride and arrogance of which nothing good can happen in your life. You have to think outside yourself. Your life and your journey is more than just about you. So don't boast, and don't brag about what you can do or have done. You will achieve greater success if you are concerned about the success of those who are watching and following you.

> *Let this mind be in you, which was also in Christ Jesus: Who, being in the form of God, thought it not robbery to be equal with God: But made himself of no reputation, and took upon him the form of a servant, and was made in the likeness of men: And being found in fashion as a man, he humbled himself, and became obedient unto death, even the death of the cross. Wherefore God also hath highly exalted him, and given him a name which is above every name: Php 2:5-9 (KJV)*

> *By humility and the fear of the LORD are riches, and honor, and life. Prov. 22:4 (KJV)*

> *Let nothing be done through strife or vainglory; but in lowliness of mind let each esteem other better than themselves. Php. 2:3 (KJV)*

> *Likewise, ye younger, submit yourselves unto the elder. Yea, all of you be subject one to another, and be clothed with humility: for God resisteth the proud, and giveth grace to the humble. 1 Pet 5:5 (KJV)*

"The man who lives for himself is a failure; the man who lives for others has achieved true success," (Norman Vincent Peale)

Integrity:

Adherence to moral principles; honesty

Whenever you are trying to do good in the sight of God, trying to represent yourself, there is also someone among you, someone in your life, in your family, on your job, at your school seeking to bring you down, and to turn you away from what you believe in. There will be seasons in your life when what you stand for and believe in is challenged. You will be tested and tempted to abandon your principles, values, and morals, and compromise your integrity. That is when you must stand firm on what you believe in. You should know what you believe in, and how you came to believe in it.

> *And the Lord said unto Satan, Hast thou considered my servant Job, that there is none like him in the earth, a perfect and upright man, one that feareth God, and escheweth evil? And still he holdeth fast his integrity, although thou movedst me against him, to destroy him without cause. Job 2:3 (KJV)*
>
> *Judge me, O Lord; for I have walked in mine integrity: I have trusted also in the Lord; therefore I shall not slide. Psalms26:1*
>
> *Blessed is the man that endureth temptation: for when he is tried, he shall receive the crown of life, which the Lord hath promised to them that love him. James 1:12*

"If you don't stand for something, you will fall for anything." (Malcolm X)

Ingredients

$\mathcal{K}$nowledge:

The sum or range of what has been perceived, discovered, or learned.

Knowledge is a key ingredient for success in any area of life. The journey towards success begins with the knowledge that you possess the necessary skills to achieve success. Knowledge is power. It empowers you to be able get the job done with confidence. Knowledge of your purpose and role in any setting or environment you encounter on your journey provides an awareness of what is needed to accomplish the task at hand. The journey towards success begins with the knowledge that you possess the necessary skills to achieve success.

> *A wise man is strong; yea, a man of knowledge increaseth strength. Proverbs 24:5*
>
> *My people are destroyed for lack of knowledge: because thou hast rejected knowledge, I will also reject thee, that thou shalt be no priest to me: seeing thou hast forgotten the law of thy God, I will also forget thy children. Hosea 4:6*

"Success is a journey, not a destination." (Ben Sweetland)

$\mathcal{L}$eadership:

The capacity or quality of being able to motivate and influence followers to respond positively to a vision, to direct, guide, instruct, and lead others.

In *Exodus 18:17-23* Moses learns about leadership from his father-in-law, Jethro. Moses had influence over the people, but he needed to learn how to lead the people. Leadership involves a vision that comes with a revelation from God. The vision gives direction for leadership. A Leader must have the ability to surround themselves with people needed to fulfill the vision; an "inner circle." Leadership also involves empowering the people around you and trusting in their ability to get the job done. The great leaders had the ability to cast their visions on to those who would follow them. The vision needs to be clearly articulated to the inner circle in order for them to implement it. When the vision is shared it motivates followers to act upon and find their role in the vision. The legacy of a leader is observed when his followers become leaders themselves. A true leader has to be able to teach, labor, and manage. People buy into the leader before they buy into the leadership. People tend to become in their life what the most important people in their life think about them. When you have a vision that orders your footsteps and those that are following you can clearly see the vision, they will want to go where you are going.

> *Then I told them of the hand of my God which was good upon me; as also the king's words that he had spoken unto me. And they said, Let us rise up and build. So they straightened their hands for this good work. Nehemiah 2:18*

> *And a vision appeared to Paul in the night; There stood a man of Macedonia, and prayed him, saying, Come over into Macedonia, and help us. And after he had seen the vision, immediately we endeavored to go into Macedonia assuredly gathering that the Lord had called us for to preach the gospel to them. Acts 16:9-10*

Ingredients

$\mathcal{M}$otivation:

Desire to do; interest or drive; that which give purpose and direction to behavior; incentive or inducement such as the fear of punishment or the expectation of reward.

When disappointments in your life create seemingly insurmountable circumstances, you need motivation to continue on in life; to continue your pursuit of your goals, happiness, success, prosperity, or whatever it is you desire. God's children suffered bondage, great afflictions, and oppression, yet one word from God (promise/expectation), motivated them to overcome their circumstances and press forward toward their goal. You may not know what lies ahead, but you know what's behind you. If you do not want to continue to experience the suffering, affliction, oppression, limitation, lack, you name it; in your life, find the motivation that causes you to pursue your dreams.

> *I am the Lord, and I will bring you out from under the burdens*
> *of the Egyptians, and I will rid you out of their bondage, and*
> *I will redeem you with a stretched out arm, and with great*
> *judgements:*
> *And I will take you to me for a people, and I will be to you a*
> *God: and ye shall know that I am the Lord your God, which*
> *bringeth you out from under the burdens of the Egyptians.*
> *And I will bring you in unto the land, concerning which I did*
> *swear to give to Abraham, to Isaac, to Joseph; and I will give it to*
> *you for an inheritance: I am the Lord. Exodus 6: 6-8*

Obedience:

The trait of being willing to obey; dutiful or submissive behavior with respect to another person.

Obedience is a learned behavior. You can learn it through trials, tribulations, and situations, or you can learn it through revelation. Delayed obedience is disobedience. This path to obedience is where you encounter unnecessary trials, tribulation, and situations. Jesus said that in this world you are going to suffer trials (John 16:33). However, it is through obedience to those who have authority in your life, whether it is a parent, a teacher, or an employer, that you achieve success in life. As you embark on your journey toward success in life, you will suffer setbacks, opposition, or maybe even those who will try to distract you. Those things challenge your obedience to the will of God and the purpose He has for your life. Obedience learned through revelation of God's purpose for your life, and the role others have in your life as you journey toward success will minimize the trials and tribulations you encounter.

> *Though he were a Son, yet learned obedience by the things which he suffered;*
> *And being made perfect, he became the author of eternal salvation unto all them that obey him;*
> *Hebrews 5: 8-9*
>
> *And being found in fashion of man, he humbled himself, and became obedient unto death, even the death of the cross.*
> *Philippians 2:8*

Ingredients

Patience:

The state of endurance under difficult circumstances, which can mean persevering in the face of delay or provocation without acting on annoyance/anger in a negative way; or exhibiting forbearance when under strain, especially when faced with longer-term difficulties

It takes patience to stay in the will of God for your life. When God gives you a revelation of the plan He has for your life, it comes suddenly; and just as suddenly as it comes, we expect a sudden manifestation of it. But God doesn't reveal the whole thing to us; He doesn't reveal all that we must go through. Without patience we get caught in all the snares, and traps that await those who want to accomplish things swiftly, and outside of God's timeframe. It is hard to exhibit patience when you want to escape the discomforts of present circumstances. You want results now; especially in today's world. We do not want to wait on success. Many people want success, but do not want to put the effort and time in required to achieve success.

> *My brethren, count it all joy when ye fall into divers temptations; knowing this, that the trying of your faith worketh patience. But let patience have her perfect work, that ye maybe perfect and entire, wanting nothing.*
> *James 1: 2-4*

> *For ye have need of patience, that, after ye have done the will of God, ye might receive the promise.*
> *Hebrews 10:36*

> *Wherefore seeing we also are compassed about with so great a cloud of witnesses, let us lay aside every weight, and the sin which doth so easily beset us, and let us run with patience the race that is set before us. Hebrews 12:1*

*P*erseverance:

Steady persistence in adhering to a course of action, a belief, or a purpose, withstanding discouragement or difficulty; persistence

Perseverance often requires patience. Sometimes you are going to have to just outlast the difficult circumstances you encounter on your journey towards success. You have to stay in the press; fight the good fight. Whatever it is that you have been called to do, or you desire to achieve in life, it will not come without adversity, challenges, trials and tribulation. Do not give up, God has a plan for you; stick to your plan. You must persevere until you achieve the success you desire.

> *I press toward the mark for the prize of the high calling of God in Christ Jesus. Phillipians 3:14*
>
> *These things I have spoken to you, that in me ye might have peace. In this world ye shall have tribulation: but be of good cheer; I have overcome the world. John 16:33*

Ingredients

$\mathcal{P}$ersistence:

The quality of persisting; tenacity; refusing to give up or let go.

There is a reward for your persistence; and that reward is honor. Honor comes to those who never give up on the pursuit of their dreams, their goals, and their destiny. When you stand up against the adversity and challenges that arise during your journey of life and success, and you overcome them, defeat them, or sometimes you just outlast them, you bring honor into your life. Never give up when things get hard. Find that resolve deep down within you that says I will not be defeated. You may not have all the answers to your problems; and you feel like throwing your hands in the air and saying, I give up. Do not give up! Be persistent. Fight for your dreams. Press forward toward your goals.

> *And I looked, and rose up, and said unto the nobles, and to the rulers, and to the rest of the people, Be not ye afraid of them: remember the Lord, which is great and terrible, and fight for your brethren, your sons, and your daughters, your wives, and your houses. Nehemiah 4:14*

> *To them who by persistence in well doing seek for glory and honor and immortality, eternal life:*
> *Romans 2:7*

> *Brethren, I count not myself to have apprehended: but this one thing I do, forgetting those things which are behind, and reaching forth unto those things which are before, I press toward the mark for the prize of the high calling of God in Christ Jesus.*
> *Phillipians 3:13-14*

Reliability:

Capable of being relied on; dependable

Reliability can bring you favor. When you can be relied upon to do what is expected of you, opportunities are afforded to you that no one else is trusted with. The parable of the ten talents in the book of Matthew sums it up quite well:

> *"For the kingdom of heaven is like a man traveling to a far*
> *country, who called his own servants and delivered his goods*
> *to them. And to one he gave five talents, to another two, and*
> *to another one, to each according to his own ability; and*
> *immediately he went on a journey. Then he who had received the*
> *five talents went and traded with them, and made another five*
> *talents. And likewise he who had received two gained two more*
> *also. But he who had received one went and dug in the ground,*
> *and hid his lord's money. After a long time the lord of those*
> *servants came and settled accounts with them. "So he who had*
> *received five talents came and brought five other talents, saying,*
> *'Lord, you delivered to me five talents; look, I have gained five*
> *more talents besides them.' His lord said to him, 'Well done,*
> *good and faithful servant; you were faithful over a few things,*
> *I will make you ruler over many things. Enter into the joy of*
> *your lord.' He also who had received two talents came and said,*
> *'Lord, you delivered to me two talents; look, I have gained two*
> *more talents besides them.' His lord said to him, 'Well done,*
> *good and faithful servant; you have been faithful over a few*
> *things, I will make you ruler over many things. Enter into the joy*
> *of your lord.' (Matthew 25: 14-23)*

espect:

Willingness to show consideration or appreciation; an attitude of deference, admiration, or esteem; regard

Respect is an ingredient that you must possess on your journey through life. Your willingness to show consideration or appreciation (respect) for someone else is as important, if not more important, than earning the respect of others toward yourself. When you have respect for others, it allows you to receive wise council and direction from them that could guide you on your journey.

> *When they heard this, they were furious and plotted to kill them.*
> *Then one in the council stood up, a Pharisee named Gamaliel,*
> *a teacher of the law held in respect by all the people, and*
> *commanded them to put the apostles outside for a little while.*
> *And he said to them: "Men of Israel, take heed to yourselves what*
> *you intend to do regarding these men. Acts 5:33-35*

Responsibility:

The ability or authority to act or decide on one's own, without supervision; The obligation to carry forward an assigned task to a successful conclusion.

With responsibility goes authority to direct and take the necessary action to ensure success. The level of success you achieve in life is influenced by the level of responsibility you demonstrate. The level of responsibility you demonstrate during various stages of your life will determine what opportunities you will be allowed at the next level of your journey. If you do not demonstrate responsibility on a current level, you can never expect to be given an opportunity to demonstrate it at a higher level.

Resiliency:

The ability to spring back from and successfully adapt to adversity. The physical property of a material that can return to its original shape or position after deformation that does not exceed its elastic limit.

You ever go through some though seasons in your life when you feel like you are being tested, tried, and stretched beyond your limit; and you feel like it's never going to end? It is at your breaking point where resiliency is a necessary ingredient to possess. When you have been hit with everything life has to through at you, and you have been knocked down a few times, but not out, you have to have a bounce-back in your spirit. You have to be able to keep standing in the face of your opposition and adversity. You must possess the ability to be able to be stretched beyond your known limitations prior to moving into your next season of promotion.

What you cannot withstand in your current level will almost certainly cause you to fail at a higher level.

Sacrifice:

Forfeiture of something highly valued for the sake of one considered to have a greater value or claim.

> *The young man said to Him, "All these things I have kept from my youth. What do I still lack?" Jesus said to him, "If you want to be perfect, go, sell what you have and give to the poor, and you will have treasure in heaven; and come, follow Me." But when the young man heard that saying, he went away sorrowful, for he had great possessions. Matthew 19:20-22*
>
> *And everyone who has left houses or brothers or sisters or father or mother or wife or children or lands, for My name's sake, shall receive a hundredfold, and inherit eternal life. Matthew 19:29*

Success comes with a price tag called sacrifice. Are you willing to make sacrifices to achieve the success you desire? Your sacrifice is the price you pay to be successful. The price you pay today matures the harvest tomorrow. Sacrifice is trading in something good for something better. Nothing is sacrifice unless it cost you something. The level of success you achieve will reflect the degree of your sacrifice.

Ingredients

$\mathcal{S}$elf-awareness:

Having knowledge or cognizance of your identity, source, and purpose.

> *And God said, let us make man in our own image, after our*
> *likeness: and let them have dominion over the fish of the sea, and*
> *the fowl of the air, and over the cattle, and over all the earth,*
> *and over every creeping thing that creepeth upon the earth.*
> *So God created man in His own image, in the image of*
> *God created he him; male and female created he them.*
> *Genesis 1:26-27*

When you try to establish your own identity, to be your own man, to be unique; when you think you are in control of your destiny most of your life, everything you try to accomplish and achieve what you believe would lead you to success, will only have short-lived success, or none at all. You must be aware of the true man in the glass. The many short-lived successes that come with a pat on the back along the journey to create your own identity, only allow the man or woman in the glass to see what you want.

When you realize that it is not the world or the person in the mirror that gives your identity; but the fact that you were created in the image and likeness of God, you finally establish self-awareness and establish your identity. God is your source. He has a plan and a purpose for your life.

You will never exercise authority above how you see yourself. You must see yourself as God sees you. You do not want your image blurred.

$\mathcal{S}$elf-esteem:

A feeling of self-respect and personal worth.

> *Then God said, "Let Us make man in Our image, according to Our likeness; let them have dominion over the fish of the sea, over the birds of the air, and over the cattle, over all the earth and over every creeping thing that creeps on the earth."*
> *Genesis 1:26*

> *When I look at your heavens, the creation of your fingers, the moon and the stars that you have set in place—What is a mortal that you remember him or the Son of Man that you take care of him?*
> *You have made him a little lower than yourself. You have crowned him with glory and honor.*
> *You have made him rule what your hands created. You have put everything under his control: all the sheep and cattle, the wild animals, the birds, the fish, whatever swims in the currents of the seas. Psalms 8:3-8*

I have come to believe that on your journey toward success in life, you are going to need a healthy self-esteem. A healthy self-esteem comes from knowing who you are, and being confident with who you are. Your self-esteem can be strengthened or destroyed by the words spoken over you during the course of your life. When you walk in the confidence of knowing God created you in His image and His likeness, there is nothing that can stop you from succeeding in life. You gain the confidence to overcome adversity in your life, and a feeling of self-respect and empowerment.

Ingredients

Understanding:

The quality or condition of one who understands; comprehension. Characterized by or having comprehension, good sense, or discernment

Choose wise, understanding, and knowledgeable men from among your tribes, and I will make them heads over you.
Deuteronomy 1:13

A wise man will hear and increase learning, And a man of understanding will attain wise counsel,
Proverbs 1:5

A scorner seeks wisdom, and finds it not: but knowledge is easy unto him that understandeth. Proverbs 14:6

Teach me, O LORD, the way of Your statutes, And I shall keep it to the end. Give me understanding, and I shall keep Your law; Indeed, I shall observe it with my whole heart.

Understanding surpasses knowledge. You can be told to do something, and even taught how to do it. All you have to do is do what you have been told. But if you do not understand it, you will not be able to teach it to someone else. Having knowledge only indicates you have good short term memory; the ability to recall what you have heard, seen, or been taught. Making an A on a test indicates that you have the ability to recall the right answers to the questions. Understanding takes knowledge to the next level. It is more than just recalling the right answers to questions; it is the application of the knowledge in real world situations. And that requires understanding of the knowledge you have learned. It is an essential ingredient if you want to achieve success in your life. Having understanding will lead to you being place in a position of leadership and authority.

I don't know everything; but I understand a lot. Knowledge without understanding is limited in its application.

**alues:**

beliefs of a person or social group in which they have an emotional investment (either for or against something); any cognitive content held as true.

> *But Daniel purposed in his heart that he would not defile himself with the portion of the king's delicacies, nor with the wine which he drank; therefore he requested of the chief of the eunuchs that he might not defile himself. Daniel 1:8*
>
> *Now the king went to his palace and spent the night fasting; and no musicians were brought before him. Also his sleep went from him. Then the king arose very early in the morning and went in haste to the den of lions. And when he came to the den, he cried out with a lamenting voice to Daniel. The king spoke, saying to Daniel, "Daniel, servant of the living God, has your God, whom you serve continually, been able to deliver you from the lions?" Then Daniel said to the king, "O king, live forever! My God sent His angel and shut the lions' mouths, so that they have not hurt me, because I was found innocent before Him; and also, O king, I have done no wrong before you."*
> *Now the king was exceedingly glad for him, and commanded that they should take Daniel up out of the den. So Daniel was taken up out of the den, and no injury whatever was found on him, because he believed in his God. Daniel 6:18-23*

Values permeate your life. It is important to ask yourself how strongly you feel about these values in your own life and about them in general and whether you are open to changing them. You might also want to think about how you came to have these values. Did you choose them consciously after careful thought? Did they come to you from your family, your friends, or from a cultural group to which you belong? Did you accept them more or less uncritically? Perhaps you are not really sure where they came from and why you hold them. That is fine, but you may want to think critically about them before they are challenged.

Ingredients

When your values are challenged you need to be able to stand firm on what you believe in. You should not allow yourself to be swayed by false doctrines that conflict with what you believe to be true. When you stand firm on what you believe in and know in your heart that it is sound doctrine, your enemies cannot hurt you, and favor and promotion are in store for you.

Vision:

Unusual competence in discernment or perception; intelligent foresight. The manner in which one sees or conceives of something. A mental image by the imagination.

Without vision, you cannot see what is in your future. Your future looks dim, and rather than pressing into your future, you begin to lie down on the job. Having vision gives you direction in life. It orders your footsteps. Vision is like a lighthouse that guides ships through adverse conditions so that they can reach their destination. Vision allows you to see where you are going and what lies ahead. Vision is for where you are going, not where you are. Your destiny will be determined by how great your vision is. Where you see yourself is where you will end up. Where you are does not define where you are going. Your vision doesn't depend on your money; your money depends on your vision.

Joseph had a vision:

> *And Joseph dreamed a dream, and he told it his brethren: and they hated him yet the more.*
> *And he said unto them, Hear, I pray you, this dream which I have dreamed:*
> *For, behold, we were binding sheaves in the field, and, lo, my sheaf arose, and also stood upright; and, behold, your sheaves stood round about, and made obeisance to my sheaf.*
> *And his brethren said to him, Shalt thou indeed reign over us? or shalt thou indeed have dominion over us? And they hated him yet the more for his dreams, and for his words.*
> *And he dreamed yet another dream, and told it his brethren, and said, Behold, I have dreamed a dream more; and, behold, the sun and the moon and the eleven stars made obeisance to me.*
> *And he told it to his father, and to his brethren: and his father rebuked him, and said unto him, What is this dream that thou hast dreamed? Shall I and thy mother and thy brethren indeed come to bow down ourselves to thee to the earth? Genesis 37:5-10*

Ingredients

And it came to pass at that time, while Eli was lying down in his place, and when his eyes had begun to grow so dim that he could not see . . . 1 Samuel 3:2

Where there is no vision, the people perish: but he that keepeth the law, happy is he. Proverbs 29:17-19

Now I am come to make thee understand what shall befall thy people in the latter days: for yet the vision is for many days. Daniel 10:13-15

Let them alone: they be blind leaders of the blind. And if the blind lead the blind, both shall fall into the ditch. Matthew 15:13-15

$\mathcal{W}$illingness:

Cheerful readiness to do something.

If you have tried to do something and you have failed, you are not a failure. You simply have not tried hard enough to be successful. If you desire to be successful at something, and you are willing to do what it takes to be successful at it, you will be successful. Do not give up and do not be discouraged. You are not a failure. Failure often times precedes success. In order to achieve success, you must be determined and committed to success. Success comes with a price tag called sacrifice. Are you willing to make sacrifices to achieve the success you desire?

Desire and willingness require sacrifice. What are you willing to sacrifice to achieve what you desire? When you want to grow, you do what you never did to get what you never had. There is nothing you cannot do, only things you have not done yet.

> *Now finish the work, so that your eager willingness to do it may*
> *be matched by your completion of it, according to your means.*
> *For if the willingness is there, the gift is acceptable according*
> *to what one has, not according to what one does not have.*
> *2 Corinthians 8:11-12*

Ingredients

$\mathcal{W}$isdom:

The sum of all knowledge learned through life experience.

Remember when you were young? You didn't ever take the time to hear what older people had to say. You would always say that old people didn't know what they were talking about. You may have mocked the old men and called them crazy, among other things. If you were willing to listen to the older generation, you may not have understood what they saying. But as you grow older yourself, you learned that that generation had acquired knowledge over the years of their lives that you did not have. Wisdom is not just the acquisition of knowledge learned, but also understanding of the knowledge. The exhibition of the understanding of the knowledge, applied to the appropriate circumstances at the appropriate times is the indication of wisdom.

Knowledge > Understanding > Wisdom

> *"Wisdom is better than strength. Nevertheless the poor man's wisdom is despised, And his words are not heard. Words of the wise, spoken quietly, should be heard, Rather than the shout of a ruler of fools. Wisdom is better than weapons of war; But one sinner destroys much good." Ecclesiastes 9:16-18*

> *Get wisdom! Get understanding! Do not forget, nor turn away from the words of my mouth.*
> *Do not forsake her, and she will preserve you; Love her, and she will keep you. Wisdom is the principal thing; Therefore get wisdom. And in all your getting, get understanding. Proverbs 4:5-7*

> *By pride comes nothing but strife, but with the well-advised is wisdom. Proverbs 13:10*

ℱruits of the Spirit

I say then: Walk in the Spirit, and you shall not fulfill the lust of the flesh. For the flesh lusts against the Spirit, and the Spirit against the flesh; and these are contrary to one another, so that you do not do the things that you wish. But if you are led by the Spirit, you are not under the law. Now the works of the flesh are evident, which are: adultery, fornication, uncleanness, lewdness, idolatry, sorcery, hatred, contentions, jealousies, outbursts of wrath, selfish ambitions, dissensions, heresies, envy, murder, drunkenness, revelries, and the like; of which I tell you beforehand, just as I also told you in time past, that those who practice such things will not inherit the kingdom of God. But the fruit of the Spirit is love, joy, peace, longsuffering, kindness, goodness, faithfulness, gentleness, self-control. Against such there is no law. And those who are Christ's have crucified the flesh with its passions and desires. If we live in the Spirit, let us also walk in the Spirit. Let us not become conceited, provoking one another, envying one another. Galatians 5:16-26

Therefore, brethren, be even more diligent to make your call and election sure, for if you do these things you will never stumble; for so an entrance will be supplied to you abundantly into the everlasting kingdom of our Lord and Savior Jesus Christ. 2 Peter 1:10-11

Change isn't change until you change your thinking. Where ever you go you take you with you. Changing environments and surrounding often is a necessary beginning for change as you pursue success on your journey through life. However, when you acquire and begin to apply the ingredient of adaptability, you must be aware of who you are deep down on the inside. Knowledge of who you are, or lack thereof, will have an impact on true and long lasting change. You can change your environment. You can change your appearance. You can change your associations. You can change the way you talk. Your behavior can even appear to be improved. You may even be having better results in your

Ingredients

life. These are all superficial surface changes. The real you is the you that will eventually manifest over time. You cannot escape adversity on your journey through life. Superficial changes only last but for so long. The real you will eventually find you. If you did not handle adversity adequately before any of those superficial changes, you will not handle them when the real you catches up to you. You can fool everyone else, but you cannot fool you.

> *"When an unclean spirit goes out of a man, he goes through dry places, seeking rest, and finds none. Then he says, 'I will return to my house from which I came.' And when he comes, he finds it empty, swept, and put in order. Then he goes and takes with him seven other spirits more wicked than himself, and they enter and dwell there; and the last state of that man is worse than the first. So shall it also be with this wicked generation." Matthew 12: 43-45*

When your thinking changes, your behavior changes. When your behavior changes, you get different results in your life based on the information you received. Your thinking changes when you have access to new information. Sometimes adversity in life will wipe you out. Other times, adversity uses you to wipe others out. Adversity will sometimes allow you to escape into a temporary, false sense of security, only to return to catch you unprepared and unequipped with the right ingredients. Each ingredient in this book can be acquired through access to the right information.

About the Author

I graduated from Syracuse University with a Master's degree in Social Work. I designed, developed, and implemented a successful fatherhood program while working at a community action agency in Syracuse, New York, before moving to Toledo, Ohio, in 2004. I worked as a School-Based mental Health Clinician for several years. I was also the team captain of a local chapter of All Pro Dad, which I had implemented at Lincoln Academy for Boys. My passion for fathers shines through as I established RESTORE Inc. in 2006, a faith-based nonprofit organization for restoring fathers back to the head of the family through the Gospel of Jesus Christ. I cofounded the Northcoast Fatherhood Collaborative and was the Assistant Director of the Northcoast Fatherhood Initiative. I am currently the Director of Field Education and Instructor at Lourdes University Department of Social Work in Sylvania, Ohio. I have authored a faith-based curriculum for restoring fathers back to the head of the family titled "Restoration of Fathers: Restoring Fathers to Their Original Purpose and Position." I have also presented at a national conference on "God's Blueprint for Successful Fatherhood" and "The Restoration of Fathers." I serve on various boards, including the Ohio Practitioners Network for Fathers and Families (OPNFF), which is a statewide collaboration that seeks to advance a fatherhood and family agenda at the state and local level, task forces, and committees in the Toledo, Ohio, area, including the Lucas County Fatherhood Initiative Leadership Team. I was recently nominated for and received the Fatherhood Heroes Award from the White House for President Obama's National Fatherhood Initiative Campaign in 2013.